SHOEMAKER BROWN GET'S DOWN

©2018 ANDREA LISA BROWN
ILLUSTRATIONS BY DOMINANT DANSBY
EDITING BY BRIAN HEMPHILL

To order additional copies of this book, contact:
Xlibris
1-888-795-4274
www.Xlibris.com
Orders@Xlibris.com

SHOEMAKER BROWN
GET'S DOWN
LEARN HOW

How it Went Down...
Writing stories should be fun. There were six of us at our house. eight including our parents. So there was never a dull moment. That was the thought that triggered the first line of the story. I wanted fun to flow through out this tale so what better way to do that then to use rhyme

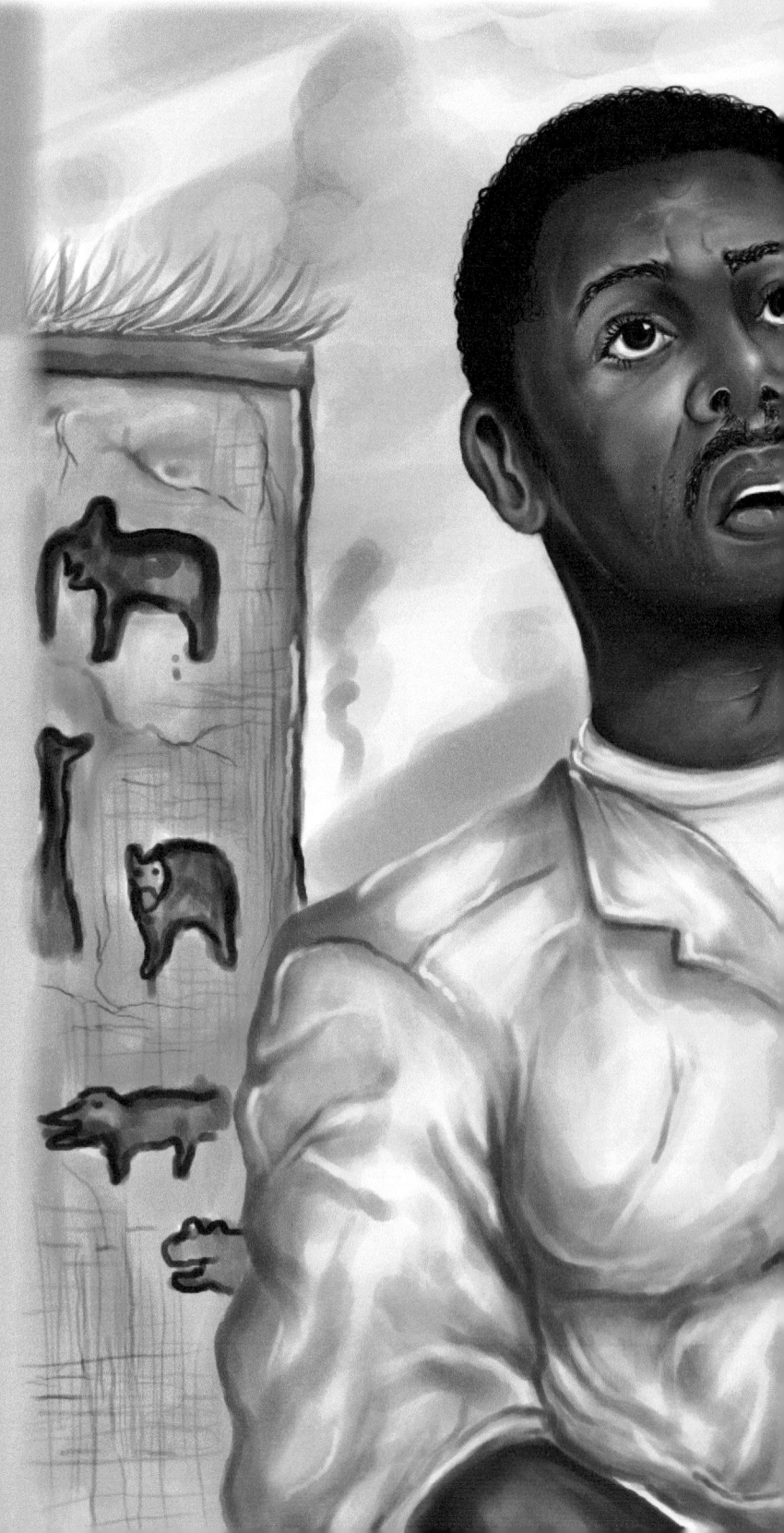

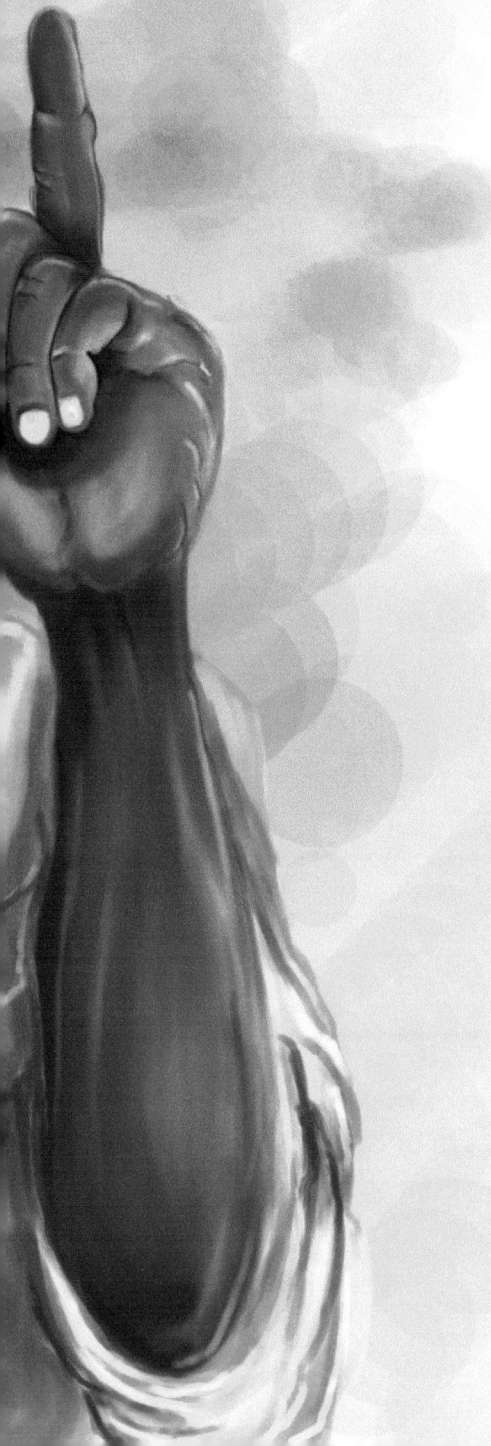

We're Bored, were bored daddy what do we do?
Well, I have an idea for all of you
Let's do a project
That will be great fun i bet
if we all work together we'll have the best time yet
Veronica tidy up our work space, Andrea grab us a snack
Tamie assist big sister toy & Pamela let baby Julious tag-along
Now for the project that we'll be working on
Those old once navy canvas shoes that I polished black
on tonight will make a big come-back

How we learned how to get down...
As you know children mimic what they see. So it wasn't odd for either of my siblings or me to dabble in making our own creations. My mother sewed also so we became very good at combining what had been displayed as their talents. Likely, making a pillow for my bed or covering an old chair were simple task!

An old once navy blue now black canvas shoe
Right before your eyes has become something new
But how you might ask?
Do things chamge so quick
Let shoemaker Brown tell you a secret
With the right tools, ambition & dedication
You can also make a creation
If you want to be a shoemaker too
A simple whack off the back of any pair will do
that makes for a fine mule shoe.

OH, DADDY, DADDY COULD IT BE
Oh Daddy, daddy look and see
Oh, Daddy, daddy do you know
Everyone can see your toes
What are you going to do Daddy
What are you going to do?

Daddy gets down...
My father was very, very good with his hands. he was the type of person that made everything. He made our bunk beds which served us through out childhood. they were in such good condition when we outgrew them that we were able to give them away to someone else. when we sat at the kitchen table, my parents sat at the ends of the table and two long benhces supported our weight on each side. Those benches were sturdy enough to support bottoms of all sizes for years and years and we didn't rid of them until a few of us had flown the nest. It was as hard to see them go as it was to leave home. The kitchen table that my father sits at in this book is very significant. It reminds me of the kitchen table that we wacthed him create so many projects during our wonder years and throughout our lives.

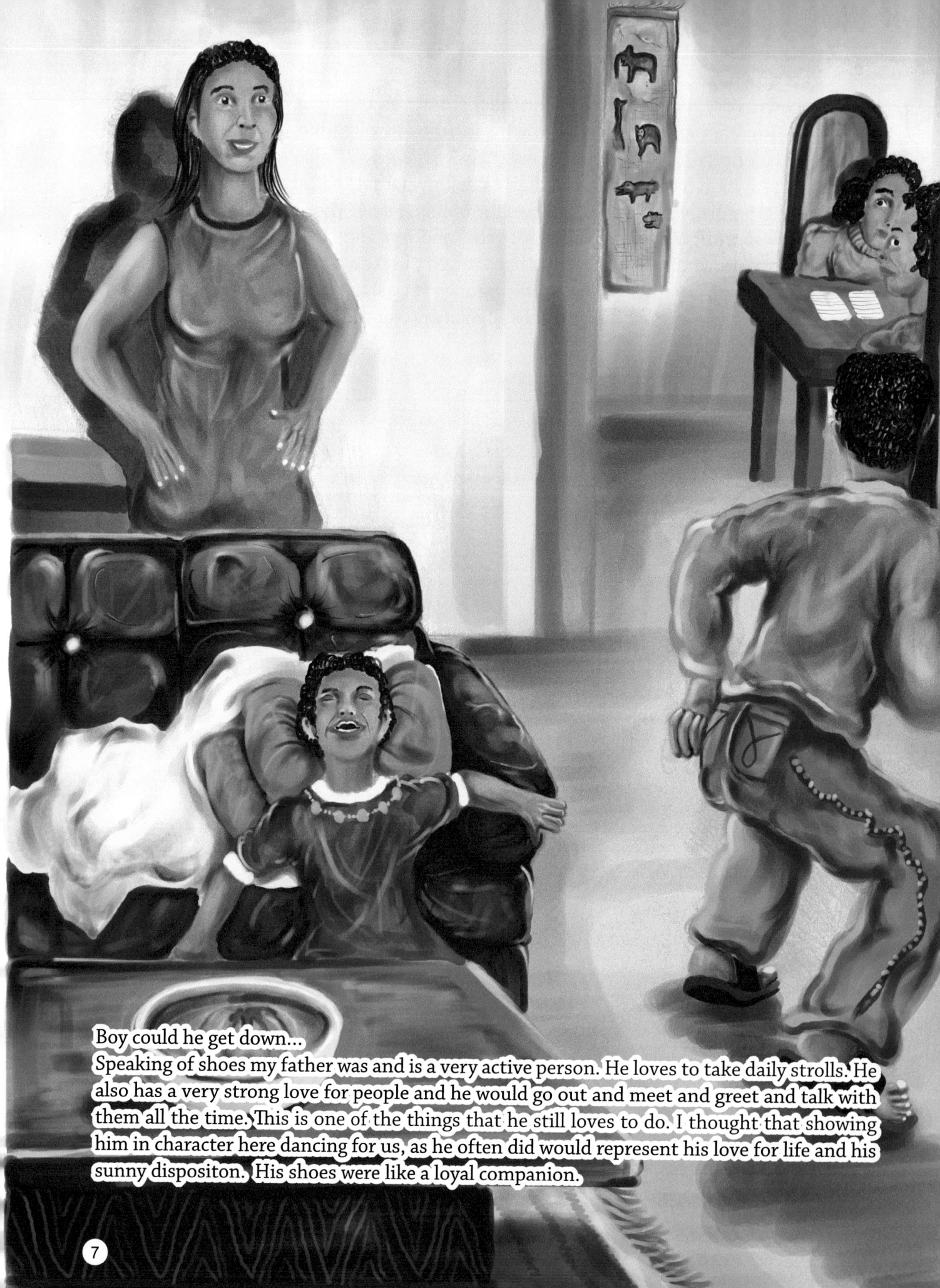

Boy could he get down...

Speaking of shoes my father was and is a very active person. He loves to take daily strolls. He also has a very strong love for people and he would go out and meet and greet and talk with them all the time. This is one of the things that he still loves to do. I thought that showing him in character here dancing for us, as he often did would represent his love for life and his sunny dispositon. His shoes were like a loyal companion.

These shoes have been through a lot
but I want them to stay
naw I'm no pack rat
but my favorite shoes are back
these shoes have been loyal, you see
in these ol comfty's i can be me

Daddy who else can multiply like you
one pair of old shoes equal two pairs of new
get down daddy, get down

Were bored, were bored daddy what do we do?
I know a way to entertain you
We can do a project
or did you forget
Get those kicks out of the closet
and let's make magic.

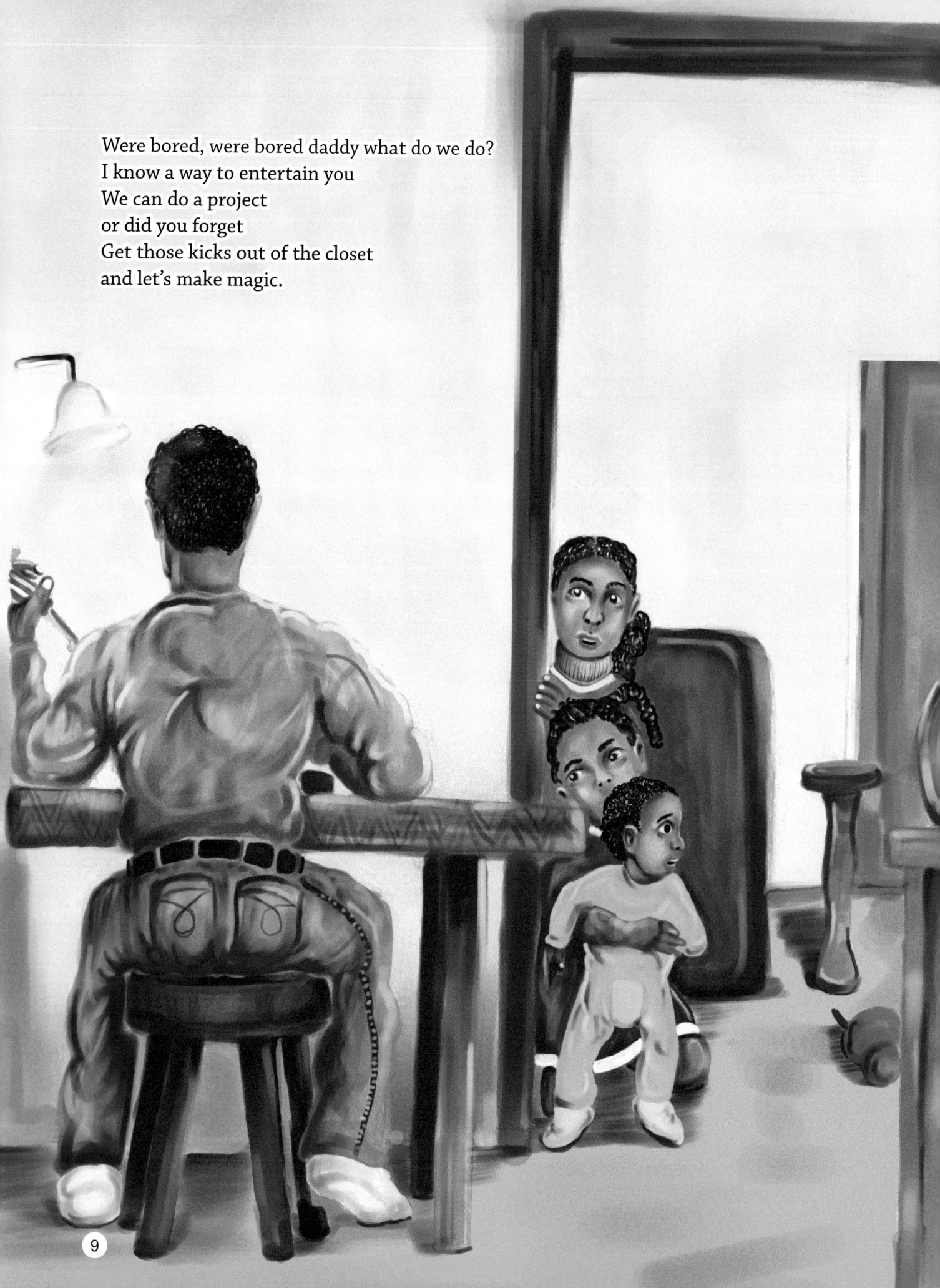

Do you want to get down...
My father was also a carpenter by trade he taught us how to do everything. Us girls would assist him in lying tiles, working on the car, interior & exterior painting, patching walls, and hanging dry wall. Light pluming and too many other things to list. we expecially enjoyed watching him drag in his treasured fines from those many, many scavenger hunts. Because of this we learned how to upolster furniture and how to repair it. We girls we very well rounded when we left our parents house. Our brother julious was the youngest child he's well equiped himself. let's just say that he did well by us by doing the absolute best they could with what they had!

(Daddy's Song)
Check out my jazzy new kicks
look at them sway
As I prance, when I dance
watch them glide as I stride
when I walk as I talk
(Our Song)
Who else can multiply like you
one pair of old shoes
equal three pairs of new
nobody but you Daddy, nobody but you

When doing that dance...
My fathers example was quite rewarding when he designed those shoes times over he was also designing our lives. I see replica's of that example in the lives and homes of my siblings all the time. It is a module that i have since utilized in the parenting of my children and i am forever grateful. children learn from what we do moreso then what we say. I am a living example of that!

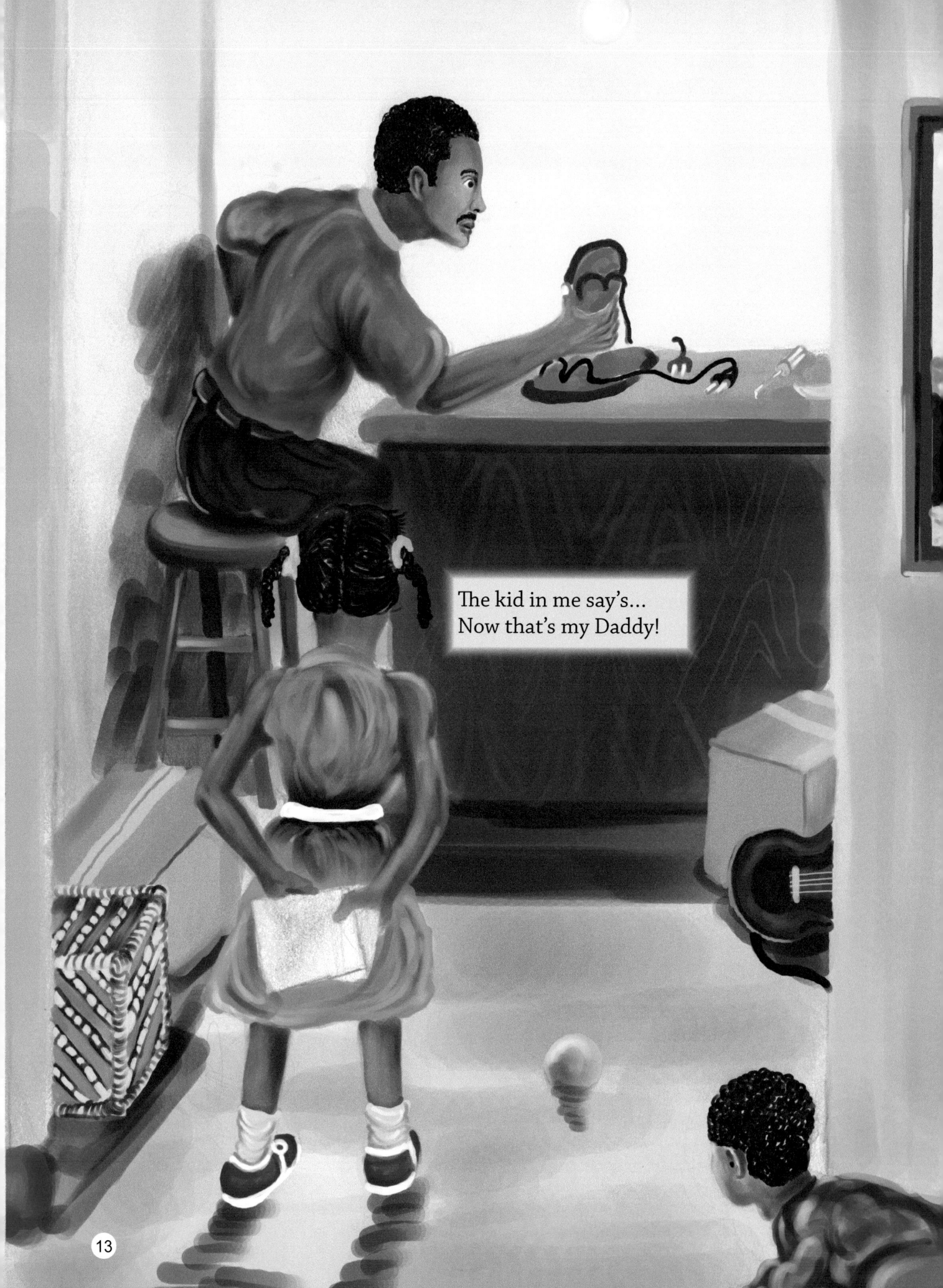

The kid in me say's...
Now that's my Daddy!

13

This is my Dad

This Is Me All Grown Up

OUR ORIGINAL STORY

"I GET TO DIG DEEP, DEEP, BACK THERE IN THE OLE CLOSET. STICK MY TOES IN MY THONG SHOES AND STROLL PROUD, DADDY, FOOTLOOSE AND FANCY-FREE!"

Summertime is just around the bend, pulling the beautiful along. I do love when summertime comes to visit. I get to feelin' a strong sense of pride. I feel like I can take even rotten lemons and make them into the sweetest lemonade. I feel I can go salvaging through life, taking the discards and making them into something so useful, something so beautiful.

Because of my dad, I am prepared. Because of his innovative nature, I am equipped and skilled enough. When I was young, way back when, there were always splashes of my father's creative talents evident around our house. But nothing, nothing stands as vivid in my thoughts as his Thong Shoes.

Thong Shoes

Magically, when I see someone in passing stroll by in a replica of your thong shoes, instantaneously I'm taken aback. The inviting warmth of home embraces me. The comforting faces of family are surrounding me. And once again, there you are, wearing that familiar grin. Your silly gestures and crazy dance have us laughing 'til our bellies ache.

"Am I with it?" you would ask.

We'd say "Yeah!"

You entertained us many days in those shoes, wearing them proudly for sometime before rebellious baby toes came popping through. But you dug out the ole sew'n' kit and beat the culprit at his own game. Stitches had their way of forcing rebels back in their places.

"Good as new?" you asked.

"Yeah!" we agreed.

But, who would have known that shortly after, little toe would somehow persuade the rest of the gang into protest with his stories of freedom. Toes forced, influenced by pressure. Pressure manipulated the weary, and the three managed to cause stitches to abandon tact. So you gave in to the inevitable, allowing those ole shoes to age gracefully.

Amazingly, grace visited only for a short spell, being made to feel unwelcome, and all. Seems she would have known that you are one who would never really give in to defeat. "All a man truly has is honor," you assured us, and you had yours to defend. Prepared for battle and with the assistance of your ole loyal companion, the utility knife, you tackled those shoes. With one whack off the back... Wham, mule shoe!

I can't remember how many years you walked around in those beloved mule shoes, nor do I recollect how many times you removed the Griffith polish off the shelf and made ash gray bow down and surrender to black. Yet never did we fret, Daddy; you were a knowledgeable man. You understood that many men tire of forceful feat, so you took up your seat at the ole workbench, humming away with your trusted friend by your side, deciding that maybe, just maybe, ten toes did deserve to be free.

And ole utility knife paved the way to glory. Hallelujah, ten toes wiggled happily in your new slippers, free as they pleased.

After parlaying around in those ole slippers for what seems like years, journey sent those shoes on to glory(so we thought). Yet, be it fate or chance, somehow such a priceless gift opted to be found, thought once to have been pushed way back in that closet, into no man's land ,,perhaps by some spiffy, new kicks. I will never forget the evening we stumbled across that pair of black/ canvas mule / slippers. You were inspired by them once again, so with your trusted friend in and hand, you removed all that was left of the ole, ash- gray canvas. Boy, were we puzzled when you **removed the last strip of what we had known as the "ole Chinese shoes"!**

Dedicated to my dad Julious C. Brown...I love you, Daddy!

THE END!

Printed in the United States
By Bookmasters